NATURE'S CHICKEN

A Book For Animal Lovers

A percentage of all proceeds from this book
go directly to benefit animals and fight animal cruelty.

by Dr. Nigel Burroughs

The Book Publishing Company
Summertown, Tennessee

© 1992 Nigel Burroughs
All rights reserved. Published in the United States by
The Book Publishing Company
P.O. Box 99
Summertown, TN 38483

Illustrations and Text by Nigel Burroughs
Design by Barbara McNew

Library of Congress Cataloging-in-Publication Data
Burroughs, Nigel, 1965-
Nature's chicken : a book for animal lovers / Nigel Burroughs.
   p. cm.
   Summary: Describes the adverse effects of factory poultry farming on human health and the chickens themselves and discusses the advantages of becoming a vegan, someone who does not eat meat or dairy products.
   ISBN 0-913990-92-2: $4.95
   1. Chickens—Juvenile literature. 2. Chicken industry—Moral and ethical aspects. 3. Animal welfare—Juvenile literature. 4. Vegetarianism—Moral and ethical aspects—Juvenile literature. [1. Chicken industry—Moral and ethical aspects. 2. Chickens. 3. Animals—Treatment. 4. Vegetarianism—Moral and ethical aspects.]
   I. Title.
HV4757.B87 1992
179'.3 dc20   92-13799
                                                          CIP
                                                          AC

ISBN 0-913990-91-4

0 9 8 7 6 5 4 3 2 1

Further copies of this book can be obtained from:
United Poultry Concerns, Inc.
P.O. Box 59367
Potomac, MD 20859

United Poultry Concerns is a non-profit information
organization addressing the use of poultry
in food production, science, education and entertainment.

In the hope that chickens will be better understood and respected by future generations.

Nigel Burroughs wrote this book at the Institute of Advanced Study, Princeton, where he was employed in mathematics research. He received his Doctorate in Mathematics from Cambridge University, England, in 1990. Nigel became a vegetarian at the age of 21, and finally gave up eating dairy products 4 years later in 1990.

This is the story of Nature's Chicken,
a peaceful bird who never harmed anyone.
In fact, people are very fond of chickens
because they lay lots of eggs.
For this reason,
they were domesticated a long time ago,
and they lived in harmony with humans for years.
The chickens were left to roam around outside, eating grass,
and scratching the ground for grain and grubs.

Spending the whole day
roaming around and scratching the ground
are things chickens love doing best.

Unfortunately things have changed.
In the last fifty years chickens have become
sadder and sadder, and all because of humans!
Fifty years ago chickens were very happy.
Every morning the roosters would get up very early
so that they could celebrate the new day
with their wonderful

"Cockle Doodle Dooooo."

But it is now very rare for the new dawn
to be met by a rooster.
They are all too sad.

Let me show you why.

It all started with a greedy farmer
who wanted to be able to keep more chickens
on less land, and pay fewer people to look after them.
He decided to keep his chickens in cages.
These cages were placed side by side and connected by
two troughs—
a trough for grain and a trough for eggs.
Whenever the chickens were hungry
they could reach through the bars and eat out of the grain trough.
Any eggs that were laid rolled down the sloping floor
and were caught in the egg trough.

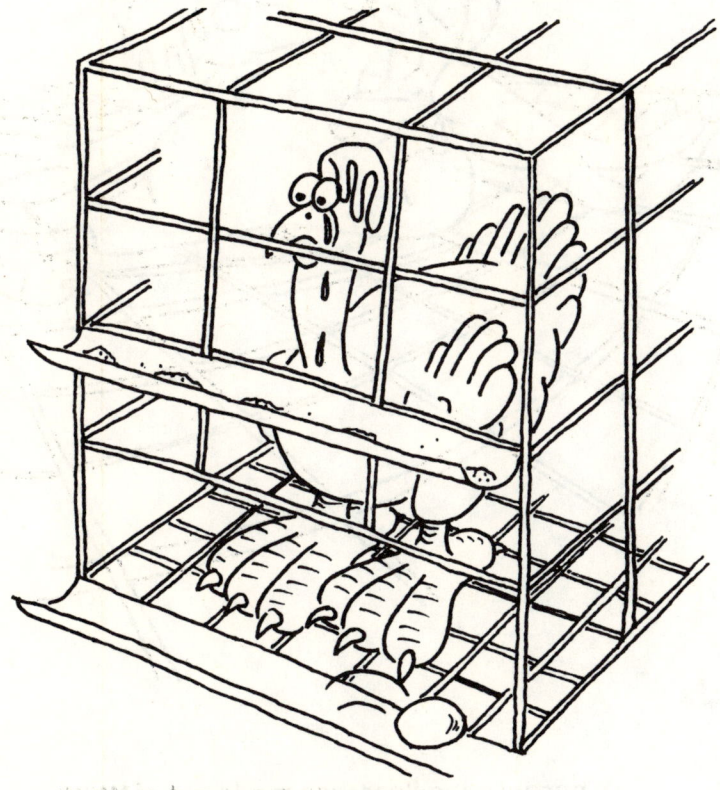

It was all very simple.
In fact, it was so simple that the farmer had nothing to do.
The farmer got rich,
because he could sell lots of eggs very cheaply.

However, the chickens were not happy.
The cages just did not feel like home.
There was nothing to do all day,
and they could not see the sun anymore
since the cages were kept in large barns.
The cages were very small and extremely uncomfortable.
In fact, they hurt their feet a lot

because the floor was made out of **wire.**

They much preferred it when they were outside running free. They often dreamed of the days when they ran about all day looking for grain and grubs. However, they could do nothing, as the farmer was much **bigger** than they were.

The other farmers became very jealous of the first farmer;
they could see how rich he was getting,
and how he could sit around all day doing nothing.
So they decided to copy him.
The other farmers were even greedier than the first.
They decided to put more hens in each cage.

In fact . . .

Not two ...

Not three ...

Not four ...

But Five!

The chickens became more unhappy.
You might think that they would appreciate some company,
being stuck in a cage all day.
But it was **SO VERY CROWDED.**
They could not even turn around or spread their wings.
If there is one thing chickens love to do,
it is to spread their wings.

So they got mad.

It was really the farmers they should have gotten mad at,
for putting them in the small cages.
But the farmers were out of reach,
and however much they squawked,
the farmers just ignored them.

So they squawked at each other.
They squawked about the lack of room,
the absence of sunshine,
the boredom of being in a cage all day,
and the farmers who would not let them out.
Sometimes they got really mad at each other
because they were always getting in each others' way,
and treading on each others' toes.
And when they got really mad, they started
to fight and peck each other.

Wouldn't you if you had a beak and were shut in a cage all day?

Well the farmers did not like this.
So they went to see their scientist friends.
"What shall we do?" they said,
"The chickens keep pecking each other."
After a few days, the scientists came back.
"Cut off their beaks," they said.
The farmers looked at each other,
and all laughed in unison,
"Yes, cut off their beaks."

So they cut off their beaks.

Chickens love their beaks.
Beaks are really useful things;
you can pick things up, peck things, and tap things.
So the chickens were even more unhappy now,
and would have stomped around in protest
if they had had the room.

The farmers thought all this was great.
They were making money,
with the possibility of an awful lot more.
But no matter how much money they made,
they never saw how unhappy the chickens were.
The money had made them blind,
blind to the cruelty they were inflicting.

Chickens were never meant to stay in cages,
and many horrible things started to go wrong.
One problem was with their toenails.
When outside, their nails get worn down by scuffling in the dirt.
But this did not happen in the cage;
their nails just grew, and grew.
In fact, they grew so much
that they sometimes got caught in the bars of the floor.
If this happened,
the chickens could not reach the food, and starved.

You might have hoped
that the farmers would take the chickens out of the cages,
and let them run around again,
scratching and scuffling on the ground.
But this was not to be so.
Instead the farmers went to see the scientists
and mumbled about "loss of profits."
The scientists replied, **"Cut off their toes."**
Some farmers liked this advice, so on their farms
they clipped the chicken's toes just behind the nail.

THIS IS CALLED TOE CLIPPING

Poor chickens.

There was no stopping the farmers now.
They were making more and more money;
it just kept flooding in. But even that was not enough.
They decided they could make even more money
if they had two types of chickens,

**one designed to lay eggs all day,
and one for the dinner table.**

In order to make as much money as possible
they wanted the laying chickens to lay as many eggs as possible,
and the dinner table chickens to grow as fat as possible
in the shortest amount of time.

So the farmers went to see their chemist friends.
"We have heard about these hormone things.
Could you give us some
to make the chickens grow faster and lay more eggs?" they said.
The chemists thought about it,
and they went to work in
their **dark** and **terrible laboratories**.

The chemists returned a month later.
"We have two hormones for you," they said,
"Here is **'FATTEROO,'** which makes the **chickens really big**,
and **'LAYUM,'** which makes **chickens lay lots of eggs**."

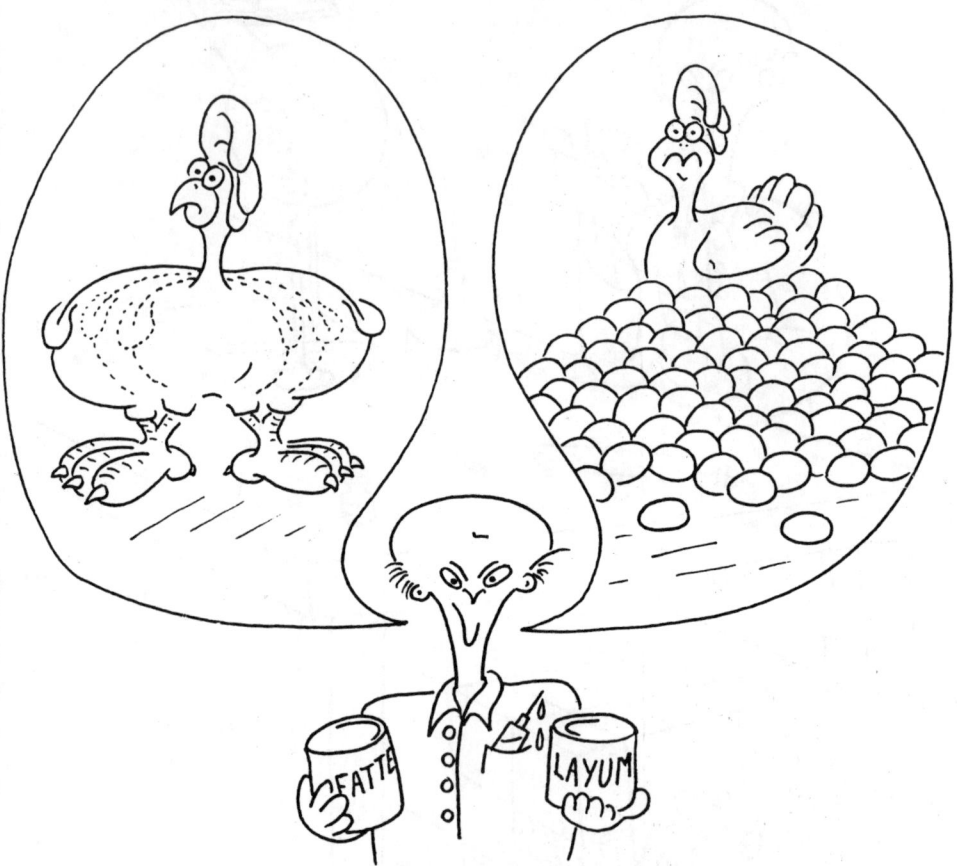

The farmers went away, happier than ever,
and put the laboratory hormones in the food.
All animals have natural hormones flowing in their bodies.
They control things like how fast you grow.
Hormones are very powerful things
and occur only in the smallest amounts.
A small amount has a large effect.
It is very important to have the correct amount of each hormone
in order to grow up strong and healthy.
Too much is not healthy for people or for other animals,
including chickens.

But the farmers were not concerned about the chickens' health;
they only wanted to make money, and lots of it, too.
So they fed the chickens **HUGE** amounts
of the laboratory hormones.
These hormones were very successful.
The chickens on **'LAYUM'** just could not stop laying,
and laid egg, after egg, after egg.
And those on **'FATTEROO'** . . .

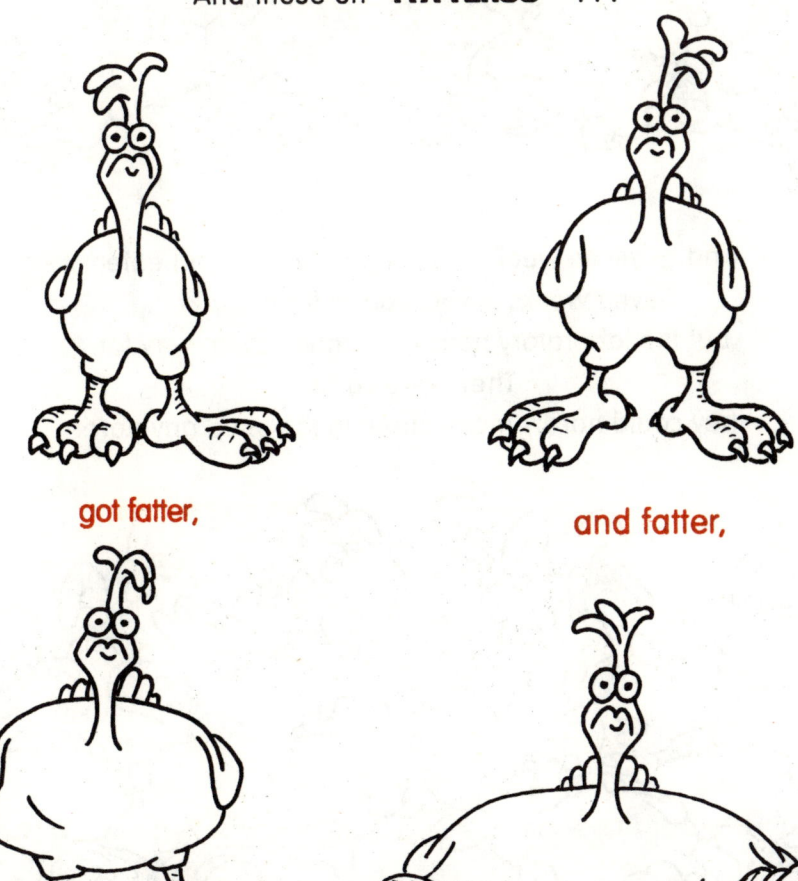

got fatter, and fatter,

and fatter and fatter.

In fact, they got so fat they could not walk anymore;
their legs were just too weak,
and sometimes broke under their great weight.

The chickens on **'FATTEROO'** grew fat very quickly.
When they hatched they were placed in huge sheds
away from their mothers.

And at seven weeks old they were sold and eaten.
Seven weeks is very young for a chicken,
but the laboratory hormones made them very fat.
They were so fat
they could hardly move about in the shed anymore.

Being fed large amounts of laboratory hormones
and squashed in a cage or shed all day is not healthy,
so the chickens soon became very ill.
The farmers ran to the chemists with their troubles
who replied, **"Feed them antibiotics."**
So the farmers fed the chickens lots of antibiotics, too.

However, the chickens were still very ill,
because the antibiotics could not cure the real problem—
lack of daylight,
lack of exercise,
and a very poor diet
with lots of laboratory hormones and other drugs.
The chickens were not as healthy as they used to be....

many went blind,

and deaf,

had broken bones,

and lost their feathers.

They all looked very sick.

These chickens are so ill
they should be staying in the animal hospital
receiving lots of love and attention until they are better.
But they aren't. They live in **FACTORY FARMS**.
As you can see,
in factory farms
they are not treated like chickens at all,
but machines;
machines to produce eggs and meat for the dinner plate.
Most of the eggs and chickens
bought in the stores come from there.

Today, many of these factory farms
are owned by huge companies
like the big drug companies and feed companies.
By owning the factory farms they can use
more of their drugs and chicken food.
They make lots of money this way.
They only care about money and not about the chickens.

Poor chickens.

Of course, all of this is a secret,
because if people knew how unhappy chickens are,
no one would buy the eggs, or eat the chickens' flesh.
Since the farmers, drug companies, and feed companies
make lots of money out of their factory farms,
they spend some
to make you all believe that the chickens are happy,
and that it is healthy to eat meat and eggs.
In fact, they pay people to think up catchy slogans
to make you buy even more, such as

"Go to work on an egg" and **"Chicken Heaven."**

But you should not believe them . . . .

CHICKENS ARE VERY MISERABLE.

Unfortunately the chicken is not alone.
Today there are many types of factory farms,
ones for ...

pigs,

cows,

ducks,

and turkeys.

These animals are all just as sad as chickens,
and they are all treated like **machines**.

Most of the eggs, milk, and meat that people buy today
come from these nasty factory farms.
This means that millions of animals are suffering,
just so that people
can drink milk,
and eat meat,
and eggs.

These poor animals suffer throughout their WHOLE lives.
They are never happy,
and never have any fun.

But it does not have to be like this.

These animals are suffering
because people buy factory farm products.
If people refused to buy them,
then the factory farms would be forced to close down.
So to help the animals we must **STOP** people
from buying factory farm products.
Unfortunately the farmers are very rich, so they are very hard to
fight. They like their factory farms
because they make a lot of money from them,
and money makes people do extremely cruel things.
There are farms that refuse to farm the factory way,
but there aren't many left.
People who want to buy from them have to search
in lots of stores, and ask lots of questions
about how the animals are kept.

Some people do not care about animals,
and when you tell them not to buy from factory farms
they will say that it is natural for people to eat animals.
But it is not natural
to raise animals without sunshine or lots of space.
And it is not natural
to be fed large amounts of hormones and antibiotics.
These people also say that it is healthy to eat meat and eggs.
But if the animals are so sick—

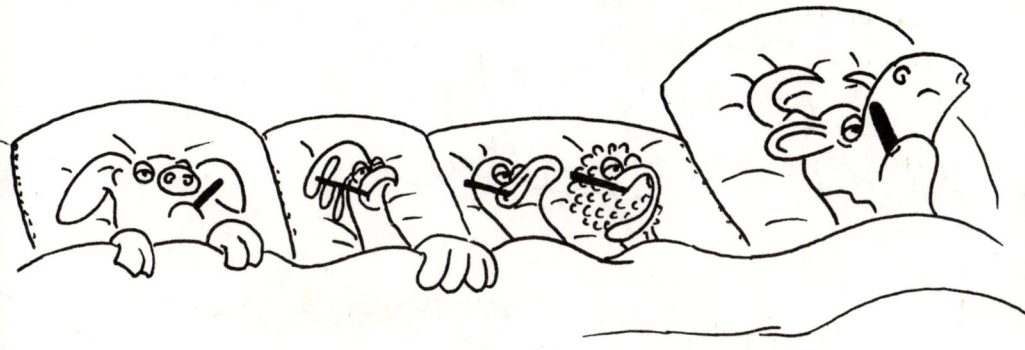

and you eat them—couldn't you get sick, too?
And if the farmers fed them
such large amounts of antibiotics and hormones,

who is eating them now?

In fact, you do not have to eat meat or dairy products at all.
You can grow up to be strong and healthy
by eating grains, fruits, and vegetables everyday.

We are not lions,
so we do not need to eat meat.

We are not babies,
so we do not need to drink milk.

And eggs are best when left with mom to hatch.

There are lots of people
who never eat meat or eggs, or drink milk.
They are called **VEGANS**.
They **never** touch any food containing animal products.
Many vegans believe it is wrong to harm or kill another animal.
They respect animals,
and try never to do anything that could harm another creature.

No animal suffers or dies because of a **VEGAN**.

Many great athletes, scientists, singers, and philosophers
are, or were, vegans.
Vegans can run and think just as well as the meat eaters,
if not even better.

Vegans eat very well, and have an exciting and varied diet.
They eat dishes from

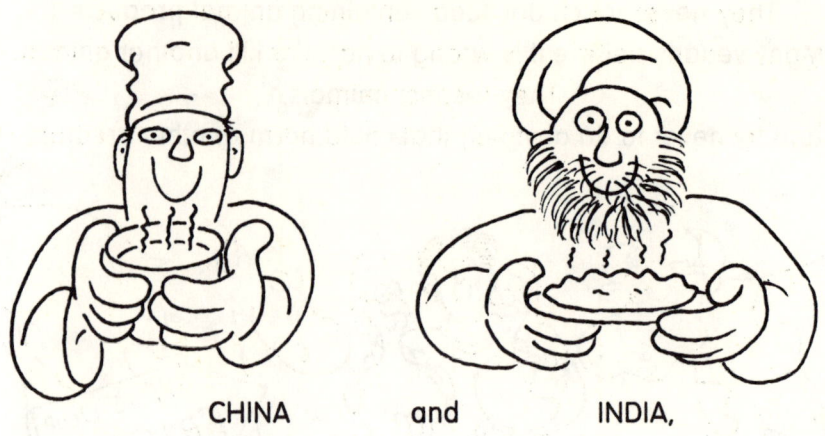

CHINA   and   INDIA,

made from tasty vegetables and grains cooked in delicious sauces.

From Greece they eat falafels and humus.
From Italy they eat pizza and pasta.
Of course the pizza is made with vegetable toppings
and no cheese,
but that is not strange in Italy!
They also eat more familiar things such as peanut butter, jelly,
spaghetti, baked beans, potatoes,
muffins, and fresh bread.

The next time someone says vegetables are dull
tell them about the soybean.
It is a very exciting little bean.

With it you can make
tofu,
soymilk,
and soy sauce.

And tofu can be used to make other wonderful things,

such as sausages,   and ice cream,

all without harming or killing a single chicken, cow, or pig.
Food is not dull when you are a vegan
because there are so many exciting ways
to enjoy meals that come from plants instead of animals.

This is what you can do to help the animals:

1. Tell people what happens to chickens in factory farms and how miserable they are. Tell them that pigs, cows, ducks, and turkeys are treated just as badly. Try to persuade them not to buy, or use, factory farm products.

2. Become a **VEGAN**; give up eating meat and dairy products. It might be hard to give them up all at once. Many people do it slowly over a few months or a year. They stop eating meat first, then after a while they stop eating dairy products. They try all the exciting foods available to vegans. Soon they feel better and so do the animals!

3. Join an organization that is helping animals. There you will meet lots of other people who love and respect animals as much as you do.

Factory Farms: A Cruel Reality

The historical development of factory farming portrayed in this story is condensed and simplified; however, the animal abuses are shown as they really are. Cramped cages and overcrowding, debeaking, and disease are a *common reality* in the factory farming of chickens.

All factory farm animals are kept in overcrowded cages, sheds, or feedlots, or isolated in stalls often so small that the animals are unable to turn around. Most of these animals are forced to live in their own feces and urine. They are fed anything from newspapers and recycled waste to meat that cannot be sold for human consumption, in particular, diseased body parts. Euthanised shelter animals can end up in this food chain. These conditions and practices promote disease—the overcrowding, terrible diet, lack of exercise, and high drug doses make the animals very susceptible to infection. The factory farm industry responds with even greater doses of vaccines and antibiotics, some of which are known to be harmful to humans.

Factory farming frustrates the natural instincts and behavior of the animals, which often results in fighting, injuries, and death. For instance, chickens have a natural tendency to peck and scratch the earth for food. The factory farm environment frustrates this behavior, so the chickens peck and scratch each other. Pigs are normally very placid animals, but the biting of each other's tails and rumps is commonly observed on the factory farm. As noted in the story, the factory farm industry responds by mutilating the animals, removing beaks and claws of chickens and turkeys, docking the tails of pigs, and dehorning cattle. These painful mutilations are performed *without anesthetics* and are done only to reduce damage that would lower profits.

Today, nearly all of the meat, milk, and eggs consumed in the U.S. come from factory farms. Packaging and promotional advertising foster the false idea of happy farm animals running free, eager to be eaten by you. No reference is made to the cruel realities of factory farming. Many egg companies abuse the term "free range," or employ ambiguous terms such as "organic" or "natural." These terms do not guarantee kindness or an absence of abuse.

Over the past 15 years, there has been an increasing volume of evidence suggesting that animal products are unnecessary for a healthy diet. In fact, many research reports imply that animal products are detrimental to health, especially in the large quantities present in the average American diet. The time has come to move away from the cruelty inherent in our lifestyle. Veganism represents a way of life that is better for both humans and animals.

Become a vegan; become cruelty free.

Everyone Can Help the Chicken

This book was written to publicize the shameful state of current U.S. animal farming methods. Only through the influence of the public can this be changed, and only through informing the public is this likely to happen. There are many organizations dedicated to this cause, and they will be willing to provide further information and answer any questions. The ideal people to contact concerning chickens or other domestic fowl is the organization dedicated to poultry:

United Poultry Concerns, Inc.
P.O. Box 59367, Potomac, MD 20859
Phone (301) 948-2406

Join United Poultry Concerns and add your voice to those already trying to help the chicken. Other organizations to contact about vegetarianism, veganism, or factory farming are:

Farm Animal Reform Movement
P.O. Box 30654, Bethesda, MD 20824
Tel. (301) 530-1737

Farm Sanctuary
P.O. Box 150
Watkins Glen, NY 14891
Tel. (607) 583-2225

Humane Farming Association
P.O. Box 3577
San Rafael, CA 94912-8902
Tel. (415) 771-2253

People for the Ethical Treatment of Animals
P.O. Box 42516
Washington, DC 20015-0516
Tel. (301) 770-7444

Physicians Committee For Responsible Medicine
P.O. Box 6322
Washington, DC 20015
Tel. (202) 686-2210

Vegetarian Resource Group
P.O. Box 1463
Baltimore, MD 21203
Tel. (410) 366-VEGE

The following books are a good source of information and background reading on the factory farm industry:

Animal Factories by Jim Mason and Peter Singer, Harmony Books/New York revised ed., 1990

Beyond Beef by Jeremy Rifkin, Dutton/New York, 1992

The Chicken Book by Page Smith and Charles Daniel, Little Brown & Co., 1975

Chicken & Egg: Who Pays the Price by Clare Druce, with an introduction by Richard Adams, Green Print (Merlin Press), UK, 1989

Diet for a New America by John Robbins, Stillpoint Publishing, 1987

For vegan and vegetarian recipes the following publications are recommended:

Cookbook for People Who Love Animals ed. by Gentle World,

Farm Vegetarian Cookbook ed. by Louise Hagler and Dorothy R. Bates, Book Publishing Co./Summertown, TN, revised ed., 1988

Instead of Chicken, Instead of Turkey by Karen Davis, United Poulty Concerns, Inc./Potomac, MD

Simply Vegan by Debra Wasserman and Reed Mangels, Vegetarian Resource Group/Baltimore,

Vegetarian Times Magazine, Paul Obis, publisher, Cowles Publications/Harrisburg, PA

Become a vegan; become cruelty free.

Ask your store to carry our fine line of books or you may order this book and other fine titles directly from:

THE BOOK PUBLISHING COMPANY
PO Box 99
Summertown, TN 38483

or call: **1-800-695-2241**

A Cooperative Method of Natural Birth Control	$ 6.95
Climate in Crisis:	
The Greenhouse Effect and What We Can Do	$11.95
Ecological Cooking: Recipes to Save the Planet	$10.95
From A Traditional Greek Kitchen	$ 9.95
George Bernard Shaw Vegetarian Cookbook	$ 8.95
Judy Brown's Guide to Natural Foods Cooking	$10.95
Kids Can Cook	$ 9.95
Murrieta Hot Springs Vegetarian Cookbook	$ 9.95
The Now & Zen Epicure	
Gourmet Cuisine for the Enlightened Palate	$17.95
The NEW Farm Vegetarian Cookbook	$ 7.95
A Physician's Slimming Guide, Neal D. Barnard, M..D.	$ 5.95
Also by Dr. Barnard:	
The Power of Your Plate	$10.95
Live Longer, Live Better (90 min. cassette)	$ 9.95
Beyond Animal Experiments (90 min. cassette)	$ 9.95
Shepherd's Purse: Organic Pest Control Handbook	$ 6.95
Spiritual Midwifery (Third Edition)	$16.95
Starting Over: Learning to Cook with Natural Foods	$10.95
The Tempeh Cookbook	$ 9.95
Ten Talents (Vegetarian Cookbook)	$18.95
Tofu Cookery	$14.95
Tofu Quick & Easy	$ 6.95
The TVP Cookbook	$ 6.95
Uprisings: The Whole Grain Bakers' Book	$13.95
Vegetarian Cooking for Diabetics	$10.95

Please add $1.50 per book for shipping.